W9-BWE-890

3- 911363

j362.29
PER

14.95

Perry, Robert
    Focus on nicotine and
caffeine

911363

j362.29
PER

14.95

Perry, Robert
    Focus on nicotine and
caffeine

Focus on Nicotine and Caffeine

Focus on Nicotine and Caffeine

A Drug-Alert Book

Robert Perry
Illustrated by David Neuhaus

TWENTY-FIRST CENTURY BOOKS
FREDERICK, MARYLAND

Published by
Twenty-First Century Books
38 South Market Street
Frederick, Maryland 21701

Text Copyright © 1990
Robert Perry

Illustrations Copyright © 1990
David Neuhaus

Printed in the United States of America

10 9 8 7 6 5 4 3 2 1

Library of Congress Cataloging in Publication Data

Perry, Robert
Focus on Nicotine and Caffeine
Illustrated by David Neuhaus

(A Drug-Alert Book)
Includes bibliographical references
Summary: Describes the history, effects, social aspects, and
physical dangers of using tobacco and caffeine products.
1. Tobacco habit—United States—Juvenile literature.
2. Smoking—United States—Juvenile literature.
3. Caffeine—Juvenile literature
[1. Smoking. 2. Caffeine. 3. Drugs.]
I. Neuhaus, David, ill. II. Title.
III. Series: The Drug-Alert Series.
HV5760.P47   1990
362.29'6'0973—dc20   89-20409 CIP AC
ISBN 0-941477-99-1

Table of Contents

Introduction

"Baby Saved by Miracle Drug!" "Drug Bust at Local School!" Headlines like these are often side by side in your newspaper, or you may hear them on the evening news. This is confusing. If drugs save lives, why are people arrested for having and selling them?

The word "drug" is part of the confusion. It is a word with many meanings. The drug that saves a baby's life is also called a medicine. The illegal drugs found at the local school have many names—names like pot, speed, and crack. But one name for all of these illegal drugs is dope.

Some medicines you can buy at your local drugstore or grocery store, and there are other medicines only a doctor can get for you. But whether you buy them yourself or need a doctor to order them for you, medicines are made to get you healthy when you are sick.

Dope is not for sale in any store. You can't get it from a doctor. Dope is bought from someone called a "dealer" or a "pusher" because using, buying, or selling dope is against the law. That doesn't stop some people from using dope. They say they do it to change the way they feel. Often, that means they are trying to run away from their problems. But when the dope wears off, the problems are still there—and they are often worse than before.

There are three drugs we see so often that we sometimes forget they really are drugs. These are alcohol, nicotine, and caffeine. Alcohol is in beer, wine, and liquor. Nicotine is found in cigarettes, cigars, pipe tobacco, and other tobacco products. Caffeine is in coffee, tea, soft drinks, and chocolate. These three drugs are legal. They are sold in stores. But that doesn't mean they are always safe to use. Alcohol and nicotine are such strong drugs that only adults are allowed to buy and use them. And most parents try to keep their children from having too much caffeine.

Marijuana, cocaine, alcohol, nicotine, caffeine, medicines: these are all drugs. All drugs are alike because they change the way our bodies and minds work. But different drugs cause different changes. Some help, and some harm. And when they aren't used properly, even helpful drugs can harm us.

Figuring all this out is not easy. That's why The Drug-Alert Books were written: so you will know why certain drugs are used, how they affect people, why they are dangerous, and what laws there are to control them.

Knowing about drugs is important. It is important to you and to all the people who care about you.

David Friedman, Ph.D.
Consulting Editor

Dr. David Friedman is Deputy Director of the Division of Preclinical Research at the National Institute on Drug Abuse.

Nicotine and Caffeine: Everyday Drugs

This is a book about drugs. Just about everywhere you turn, you hear about drugs.

You know that using drugs is a problem. You know how dangerous they are. You know how important it is for you to stay away from drugs like marijuana, alcohol, and cocaine.

But there are other drugs you may not hear so much about. You may not hear about them even though you see people use them. In one way or another, they are a part of your life even though you may never think about them.

This is a book about nicotine and caffeine. They are used by millions of people every day. But that doesn't mean they are safe to use. The fact is they *are* drugs. They change the way the body works. They change the way the brain works. They change the way people think, feel, and behave.

Like other drugs, nicotine and caffeine hurt the people who use them.

How much do you know about nicotine and caffeine? Do you know these drugs when you see them? Here is a picture of ordinary people on an ordinary day doing ordinary things. One of the ordinary things they are doing is using drugs. Can you make a list of the everyday products in this picture that contain nicotine or caffeine? Can you think of any others?

How did you do? Did you know that a cigarette contains nicotine? Or that a cup of coffee contains caffeine? These are some of the everyday things that contain nicotine or caffeine.

Here are many of the everyday products that contain nicotine or caffeine:

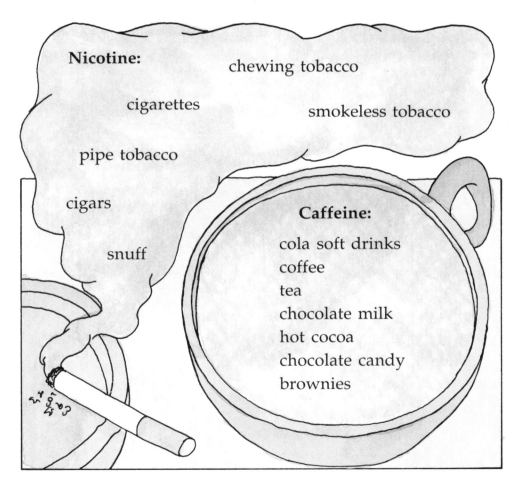

Nicotine:

chewing tobacco

cigarettes

smokeless tobacco

pipe tobacco

cigars

snuff

Caffeine:

cola soft drinks
coffee
tea
chocolate milk
hot cocoa
chocolate candy
brownies

You might ask, "What is so dangerous about a single cigarette?" Or you might not believe that a cup of coffee or a soft drink really contains a drug.

If nicotine and caffeine are such everyday drugs, can they really be that big a problem?

The answer is "Yes."

Nicotine is a very powerful and dangerous drug found in tobacco products. Tobacco products can cause heart attacks, cancer, lung diseases, and many other problems. Cigarettes and other tobacco products kill over 390,000 people a year in the United States and Canada. Using tobacco products is the number one health problem in North America. And breathing other people's smoke can be harmful, too.

Nicotine is a very addictive drug. It changes the brain so that people who use tobacco products feel that they *need* to use them. This need for drugs is called addiction. It is very hard for people who are addicted to nicotine to stop using tobacco products. People who give up smoking or stop using other tobacco products often feel sick and irritable. They may go back to using nicotine, even if they don't want to.

Nicotine is always a problem for young people. Using tobacco products is especially dangerous to growing bodies. And once young people become addicted to tobacco products, they are likely to continue to use them as adults.

Nicotine is also a gateway drug. Using tobacco products is like opening a gate to drug problems. Young people who use drugs to run away from problems or just to change the way they feel may not learn how to face life without drugs. Young people who use tobacco products are more likely to try other drugs, too.

These are some of the reasons why it is against the law for young people to buy tobacco products.

Caffeine is not as dangerous as nicotine, but it is not completely safe either. Too much caffeine causes problems for the people who use it. It makes them nervous, jittery, and easily upset. It causes headaches, upset stomachs, and sleeplessness.

Caffeine is a special problem for those young people who eat lots of candy bars and drink lots of cola sodas. It is not against the law for young people to buy products with caffeine in them, but it is easy to get too much caffeine.

Caffeine is less habit-forming than nicotine, but it is still difficult for people to stop using caffeine once they have started.

These are some of the reasons why young people need to watch how much caffeine they use.

It is important for you to know the facts about nicotine and caffeine. It is important for you to know what these drugs can do to people who use them.

But it is also important for you to be the kind of person who can say "No" when you really want to: not just to drugs, but to anything that you don't think is right or safe.

This book will give you the facts about nicotine and caffeine. You will learn what kinds of drugs they are and what they do to us. You will learn how nicotine and caffeine were used long ago and how they are used today. You will learn what kinds of decisions you will have to make as you grow up in a world of everyday drugs. And you will also learn how and why to say "No" to drugs and "Yes" to a happier and healthier life.

There are many people who will help you make the right decision about drugs. Your teachers and parents will help you to say "No." Even your friends will help you to say "No." And there is one other person who can be a big help.

That person is you.

The First Smoke: Why?

They know it's against the law. They know they can get in trouble for doing it. But many young people still want to do it.

They know their parents and teachers don't want them to do it. They know most of their friends don't want them to do it. But they still want to do it.

They know that it causes cancer and lung disease. But they still want to do it.

They know it tastes bad and smells worse. But they still want to do it.

What is "it"? "It" is smoking cigarettes or using tobacco products. Nearly one out of every five high school students smokes cigarettes. Half of them started smoking by the time they were in the eighth grade. And many of them smoked their first cigarette by the sixth grade.

The first time people smoke, they get a clear message: "Hey, this stuff is awful!" That message comes from their own bodies. Tobacco smoke burns the throat, causes coughing, and makes people dizzy. The body doesn't need it, doesn't want it, doesn't like it, and does everything it can to make that message loud and clear.

But, still, people start to smoke. The question is, "Why?"

People who start to smoke or use tobacco products don't listen to their own bodies. They don't listen to good advice. Instead, they listen to many wrong ideas about nicotine. Maybe you've heard some of these ideas, too:

"I see people who smoke. It's not hurting them."

Yes, it is. It's hurting them even if they don't feel it right away. It can take a long time to see (and feel) how dangerous some drugs are. Nicotine is like that. It may take many years for people who use tobacco products to develop cancer or other diseases. But the fact is they *are* hurting themselves. They are hurting themselves every time they smoke.

"I'll stop smoking when I feel like it."

No, you won't. You may not be able to stop smoking when you feel like it. People who use tobacco products get addicted to the nicotine in them. The fact is the younger people are when they start smoking, the harder it is for them to stop. Many people who start smoking at an early age keep smoking for the rest of their lives—lives cut short by tobacco use.

"Most kids my age smoke cigarettes."

No, they don't. It may seem to you that lots of kids your own age are smoking cigarettes or using tobacco products. But the fact is most young people never try cigarettes or tobacco in any form. Many others try it once and never do it again. And keep in mind: it is against the law for young people to buy tobacco products.

Why do young people listen to these wrong ideas? Why do they tell themselves these lies about nicotine?

Young people start to smoke because they feel pressure to do it. They feel pressure to use something they know is not right for them. They feel pressure to keep on doing something that, deep down, they don't really want to do. It must be a very strong pressure that makes young people start to smoke.

Where does this pressure come from?

Much of the pressure on young people comes from other kids who smoke. This is called peer pressure. Peer pressure means doing something to be one of the crowd. It means doing something to fit in with other kids. And, sometimes, it means doing things we would rather not do. Many young people start to smoke because they feel pressure to be like other kids. They feel pressure to be liked by other kids. And they think smoking is an answer to peer pressure.

Will Smoking Make You Popular?

Many young people try smoking to be popular. They think it helps them look "cool." They think it helps them join the "in" crowd. But think about this:

- Cigarette smoke stinks. The odor clings to your clothes and makes you smell like a stale ashtray.

- Cigarettes give you bad breath. Bad? They give you awful breath!

- Boys and girls would rather be friends with non-smokers. Studies show that most young people like to "hang out" with kids who don't smoke.

- More and more places are off-limits to people who smoke. It's a lot easier to find things to do if you don't smoke.

- Being physically fit is "in." But you're not "in" if you're poisoning your lungs with tobacco smoke.

There *is* one crowd that you can join by smoking cigarettes. You can join other kids who have become hooked on nicotine.

That's one "in" crowd you can live without.

Young people always feel pressure to be more grown up. Little children like to "dress up" as adults or play imaginary games of "Mommy" and "Daddy." Young people in elementary school want to be like the older kids they see in junior high and high schools. The older kids want to be adults. Many kids think smoking makes them look and feel more adult. They think smoking is an answer to the pressure to grow up.

Pressure to smoke may also come from adults. That may sound surprising because most adults would never want you to start smoking. But many adults do smoke, even parents and teachers who know how harmful smoking is. Young people learn by watching what adults do just as much as they learn by hearing what adults say. If they watch adults smoke a cigarette or pipe, they learn that adults say one thing but do another. They might think that smoking can't really be that harmful if so many adults are doing it. They might even think that smoking makes them more like the adults they know.

The adult world puts pressure on kids to smoke in other ways. Not only do many adults smoke, but the companies that sell cigarettes and other tobacco products make them look fun and exciting. They sell cigarettes and chewing tobacco to

young boys by making it seem that "cool" and "macho" men use tobacco products. They sell cigarettes to young girls by making it seem that glamorous and beautiful women use tobacco. You see and hear advertisements for tobacco products everywhere, and they all tell you the same thing: smoking is the thing to do. Of course, what they don't tell you is the truth. The truth is that nicotine is harmful and addictive.

These pressures are a normal part of growing up. But they can make it hard to decide for yourself what you want to do and don't want to do. As they grow up, young people often feel alone and confused. They often feel shy, unpopular, and uncertain about themselves. A cigarette may seem to be a way to build up self-confidence. It may seem to make the world a little less scary.

But nicotine won't make it easier for you to be yourself. It won't help you to make the tough decisions that all kids face as they grow up. It will only tie you to an unhealthy and unattractive habit.

Today, more and more people are learning the facts about nicotine. Every day, many people are saying "No" to nicotine. And, every day, many people who use tobacco products stop the nicotine habit. They are making a decision for themselves. They are deciding to say "No" to the pressures to use nicotine. They are saying "Yes" to healthy and drug-free lives.

What Is Nicotine?

Nicotine is a colorless, oily liquid found in the leaves of the tobacco plant. It is a very poisonous drug. If you ate even a thimbleful of nicotine, it would kill you. In fact, nicotine is so poisonous that it is used by some farmers to kill insects.

Yet this is the same drug that over 50 million people in the United States and Canada use every day.

What does this everyday drug do?

Nicotine is a kind of drug known as a stimulant. Using nicotine stimulates or speeds up the way the body and brain work. The way it makes people feel is different for different people. It gives some people more pep and energy. They say they get a "kick" from a cigarette or chewing tobacco. Some people find that nicotine gives them a calm feeling. They say it helps them to relax.

One thing about nicotine is the same for all people who use it. Nicotine is very addictive. Using nicotine changes the way the nerve cells of the brain send and receive messages. The messages to and from the brain tell us what we need to do to stay alive and healthy. When we need food, the brain tells us we are hungry. When we need sleep, the brain tells us we are tired. But when people use nicotine regularly, the brain begins to need nicotine the same way it needs food or sleep. People who use tobacco products soon feel that they must have nicotine, just as they must have food and sleep in order to stay alive. They feel a craving for more nicotine. They are addicted to it.

Most people who use tobacco smoke it. Smokers can be seen puffing away everywhere. Like little smokestacks, they send out poisonous gases into the world around them and deep into the world inside them.

Tobacco Products

Tobacco products come in many forms:

- Most people who use tobacco smoke it. Cigarettes, cigars, and pipe tobacco are made from shredded tobacco leaves. The nicotine enters the body in the tobacco smoke. Used this way, the nicotine enters the bloodstream through the lungs and is carried quickly to the brain.

- Another way to use nicotine is to chew a small wad of moist tobacco called chewing tobacco. Used this way, the nicotine enters the bloodstream through the mouth and stomach.

- Some people use a powdery form of tobacco called smokeless tobacco or snuff. Users put a pinch of smokeless tobacco in the mouth, between the gum and the cheek. Used this way, the nicotine enters the bloodstream through the soft linings of the mouth. Smokeless tobacco is one of the oldest ways to use tobacco. In the past, users would sniff a pinch of the powdery tobacco.

When tobacco is burned, it releases a number of harmful gases. Two of the most poisonous are carbon monoxide and hydrogen cyanide. It's these gases that burn the throat and lungs, irritate the eyes, upset the stomach, and make smokers feel faint and dizzy.

But they do much worse than that. The body's lungs and heart are damaged by these gases. They make it harder for the lungs to breathe. And, over time, they can cause diseases that completely shut down the body's breathing system. They make it harder for the heart to pump blood. And, over time, they can cause diseases that completely stop the flow of blood throughout the body.

In other words, these gases kill people!

Nicotine is not the only chemical found in tobacco smoke. Tobacco smoke also releases thousands of chemicals that form a gummy paste known as tar. Maybe you've seen the thick, black tar that is used to pave roads. Imagine coating your lungs with that! Well, that's exactly what smokers do. This is another cause of lung disease. Tar also causes cancer, a disease that attacks and destroys the body's healthy cells and tissues. The American Cancer Society says that the tar in cigarette smoke is the leading cause of cancer deaths.

There are brands of cigarettes that are advertised as being "low" in tar and nicotine. But they are not any safer than regular cigarettes. Smokers of these "light" cigarettes smoke more of them and inhale even more deeply. So they get as much tar and nicotine as people who smoke regular cigarettes.

Cigars, pipe tobacco, chewing tobacco, and smokeless tobacco are also harmful. They cause diseases of the mouth, throat, and stomach. And the nicotine in these tobacco products is just as addictive as the nicotine in cigarette smoke.

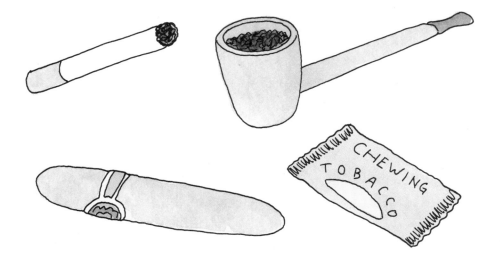

There are many tobacco products, but there is no safe way to use them. The only safe thing to do is to say "No" to the nicotine habit.

Nicotine: A History

Hundreds of years before Christopher Columbus sailed from Spain, the Indians of South and North America smoked tobacco, or "tabac" as they called it. They thought the tobacco plant, which grew wild in North and South America, was a gift from the gods. The Indians believed that tobacco worked magic and brought good luck. Chewing and smoking tobacco was an important part of their religious and social customs.

In 1492, Columbus noticed Indians carrying the dried leaves of the tobacco plant. In his diary, he wrote that the Indians placed a "high value" on the plant and "drank the smoke" of its leaves. It was not very long before the Spanish explorers began to smoke tobacco, too. One report from the New World even told of Spanish soldiers who said they could not stop smoking tobacco. It is the first written account of nicotine addiction.

Columbus took tobacco plants and seeds with him when he returned to Spain. Although some Spaniards did not like the new smoking practice, it quickly became popular. Tobacco was even used as a medicine. Soon, the wild tobacco plant of the New World was not enough to supply the nicotine needs of the Old World. Spanish colonists in the New World began to grow tobacco themselves and ship boatloads of it back to Spain. It was the beginning of the tobacco industry.

Tobacco use spread to other countries as well. Sailors from Portugal brought tobacco back from Brazil. The French ambassador to Portugal, a man named Jean Nicot, introduced tobacco to the king and queen of France. (The word "nicotine" comes from his name.) And men like Sir Walter Raleigh and John Rolfe grew tobacco in the British colony of Virginia. The taste for tobacco products was growing rapidly as more and more tobacco farms and plantations sprang up in the colonies.

In the 1600s and 1700s, growing tobacco became one of the largest industries in the British colonies. Maryland and Virginia alone grew millions of pounds of tobacco. It took thousands of slaves to plant and harvest the huge tobacco crop. The tobacco leaves were sent to England, where they were made into pipe tobacco or the more powdery snuff. These tobacco products were then sold back to the colonies.

After the American Revolution, the newly independent people of the United States grew tobacco for themselves. Now, American tobacco planters sold their crop directly to factories in the new United States. Tobacco was, at last, a completely American product.

The tobacco industry in North America continued to grow. In the early and mid 1800s, cigars and chewing tobacco became popular. Then, in the late 1880s, a new way of using tobacco caught the attention of smokers everywhere. It was a roll of shredded tobacco wrapped in paper. Many people thought it was just a passing fad. But this roll of tobacco, called a cigarette, was no passing fad. It soon became the most popular way to use tobacco. By 1900, over 5 billion cigarettes were being sold each year.

The 1900s saw the birth of the modern tobacco industry. With new machines, tobacco manufacturers were able to turn out more and more cigarettes and cigars. Advertising made smoking a part of the American way of life. Women as well as men took up the practice. And young people began to smoke in ever increasing numbers.

Today, the American tobacco industry makes over 700 billion cigarettes and over 4 billion cigars each year. Tobacco products are sold in every grocery and convenience store, and people in the United States and Canada buy over $20 billion worth of tobacco products a year. The tobacco industry now employs over 2 million people.

The history of tobacco sounds like a true success story. But not everyone thought the spread of the tobacco habit was a good thing. As long ago as the 1500s, people complained that the practice of using tobacco was unhealthy. However, it was not until the mid 1900s that scientists learned just how dangerous tobacco products really are. In the 1950s and 1960s, they observed that smokers had higher rates of lung cancer and heart disease than non-smokers did. Smokers had higher rates of death overall than non-smokers did.

In 1961, the Surgeon General of the United States, the nation's chief doctor, asked a panel of experts to study the effects of smoking on health. They made their report in 1964. Here are some of the things the 1964 Surgeon General's report on smoking cigarettes had to say:

- Smoking is a national health problem.

- Smoking is a cause of lung cancer.

- Smoking is a cause of mouth and throat cancer.

- Smoking is a cause of heart and lung diseases.

- Smoking may cause stomach and liver diseases.

- Nicotine is a habit-forming drug.

The 1964 report was the first time that the United States government said that smoking was a health problem. Other studies soon gave us even more information about the dangers of smoking. These studies showed that millions of people were hurting themselves by smoking. In 1966, the United States Congress decided to take action. Congress made the tobacco companies put a health warning on each pack of cigarettes: "Smoking can be hazardous to your health." In 1970, Congress made the warning label even tougher. It now read: "The Surgeon General has determined that cigarette smoking is dangerous to your health." There was no longer any doubt about it.

By the 1970s, it was clear that smoking was a major health risk. Congress tried to find new ways to stop tobacco use. In 1971, Congress made it illegal to advertise cigarettes and tobacco products on television and radio. Reports from the Surgeon General's office in 1972 and 1986 also showed that second-hand smoking, or breathing in other people's smoke, was dangerous to non-smokers. In the 1980s, non-smokers began to insist on their right to breathe clean air. And, today, "No Smoking" signs are seen in more and more places.

Thank You
For
Not Smoking

In 1989, on the 25th anniversary of the 1964 report on smoking and health, the Surgeon General's office released a new report on smoking. It condemned tobacco use and asked Congress to take further steps to stop people from smoking. The 1989 report said that smoking causes one out of every six deaths each year. That's 390,000 deaths a year. None of these deaths has to happen, the report said.

The report also said that people are smoking at younger ages. According to the American Medical Association, tobacco is used daily by more young people than any other drug. Over 3.5 million teenagers use tobacco products. Because nicotine is very addictive, it is likely they will go on to become adult smokers, too.

Today, smoking is a major problem for young girls and women. In fact, the number of teenage girls who smoke is going up. The 1989 report on smoking said that one out of every four teenage girls is a smoker. It is not surprising that the number of women with lung cancer and heart disease is going up, too.

But there is good news about smoking. Over 33 million Americans have quit smoking. And the number of people who smoke is going down. In 1965, 40% of adults smoked. Today, only 29% of adults smoke.

Nicotine Warning

By law, cigarette manufacturers now have to put health warnings on every cigarette pack. Each cigarette pack has one of the following warnings:

Smoking causes lung cancer, heart disease, emphysema, and may complicate pregnancy.

Quitting smoking now greatly reduces serious risks to your health.

Smoking by pregnant women may result in fetal injury, premature birth, and low birth weight.

Cigarette smoke contains carbon monoxide.

Tobacco and Illness

"Should we do this? Won't it make us sick?"
"No, it must be okay. The other kids do it all the time."
"But what about cancer?"
"Cancer? I'll worry about that when I'm 90."
"I don't know. It's bad for you."
"Being unpopular is bad for you, too. Come on."

Have you ever heard a conversation like this? It's just two kids talking together before they smoke their first cigarette. But there are millions of young people who start to smoke each year. Studies show that many of them start to smoke between the ages of 11 and 13. They may know that smoking causes lung cancer and heart disease, but they think it won't happen to them. They don't worry about it.

But they should. If they continue to smoke, they will find it very hard to stop. That's because the nicotine in tobacco products not only hurts the heart and lungs, it also changes the way the brain works. When people use tobacco on a regular basis, the brain cells begin to want a steady dose of nicotine. Smokers then need nicotine to feel normal. This need for the drug is called dependence. And there are more people dependent on nicotine than on any other drug.

If people who are dependent on nicotine do not get the drug, they go through nicotine withdrawal. Withdrawal is the sick feeling drug users have when they no longer get the drug they are used to getting. When smokers try to stop the nicotine habit, even for a very short time, they feel upset, angry, nervous, and jittery. They may not be able to sleep or think clearly. Most of all, they feel that they must have another cigarette.

The regular use of tobacco products also leads to nicotine tolerance. Tolerance means that people need more and more of a drug to get the same feeling they got when they first started using the drug. The brain builds up a tolerance to nicotine very quickly. That is why people may start out by smoking only one or two cigarettes a day, but soon find they want more—and more and more. They are soon smoking several packs of cigarettes a day. They smoke whenever and wherever they can. They are addicted to nicotine.

To understand why tobacco products are so harmful, you need to know what happens to your body when you use them. Let's find out by following a puff of cigarette smoke as it travels through the human body.

Breathing in and breathing out probably seems like the most natural thing in the world to do. Breathing in is how the body gets the oxygen it needs to live and stay healthy. The cells of the body combine oxygen with food and drink to release energy. This oxygen is in the air around us. It enters the body through the nose or mouth every time we take a breath.

Breathing out is how the body gets rid of carbon dioxide, a waste gas it no longer needs. As the body uses oxygen to make energy, it creates carbon dioxide. This waste gas then leaves the body through the nose or mouth every time we let out a breath.

The air we breathe flows down a tube called the trachea (or windpipe) and enters two pathways called bronchial tubes. The bronchial tubes branch out into smaller tubes called bronchioles. The air travels through these bronchioles until it reaches a cluster of tiny air sacs called alveoli. Oxygen passes through the alveoli and enters the bloodstream, where it is carried to every part of the body. At the same time, carbon dioxide passes out of the bloodstream. Carbon dioxide passes into the alveoli and back through the airways in the lungs.

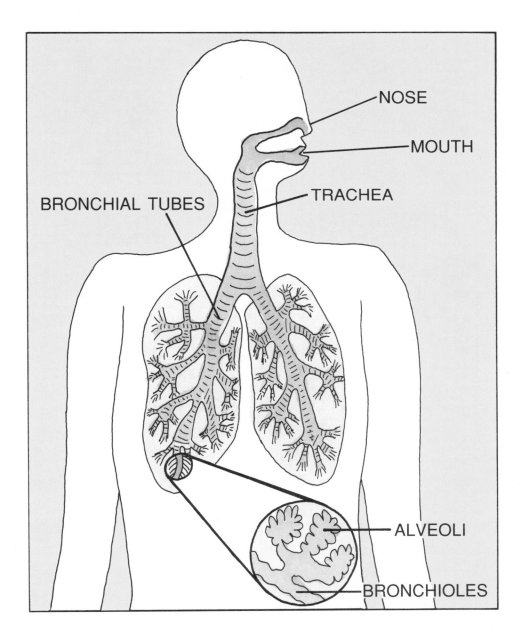

NOSE

MOUTH

TRACHEA

BRONCHIAL TUBES

ALVEOLI

BRONCHIOLES

In and out, in and out: 14 times a minute, 20,000 times a day, 515 million times in a lifetime. The lungs are effective breathing machines. They even keep themselves clean. The airways in the lungs are lined with mucus, a thick, sticky fluid that traps bits of dirt and other particles in the air that don't belong in our lungs. The cells that line the airways move the mucus and the trapped particles out of the lungs. These cells have tiny hairs called cilia that move the mucus in the same way that oars move water past a boat.

But we have to do our part to keep the lungs clean, too. There's nothing clean about breathing in cigarette smoke. And the lungs are not able to clear out tobacco tar. Cigarette smoke hurts the lungs in several ways:

- Cigarette smoke can damage the cilia that keep the lungs clean. This allows too much mucus to build up in the lungs and makes it hard to breathe.

- Cigarette smoke harms the linings of the bronchial tubes. This also causes mucus to build up in the lungs, making it hard to breathe.

- Cigarette smoke damages the alveoli. This makes it harder to get oxygen into the bloodstream.

- Cigarette smoke causes lung cancer. Cancer attacks healthy tissue and destroys the lungs.

In short, cigarette smoke keeps the lungs from doing the job they are meant to do. Even these wonderful breathing machines can break down if they are not properly cared for.

Smoking cigarettes can also damage the heart. Smoking makes the heart beat faster and work harder to pump oxygen throughout the body. Over many years, this can put too much of a strain on the heart and cause heart disease. Smoking also disrupts the easy flow of blood throughout the body. It can add to the risk that blood vessels may become blocked (blood clots) or even burst (stroke).

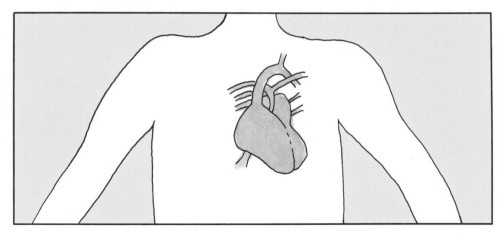

Cigarette smoke causes many other problems. Smoking causes cancers of the mouth, throat, esophagus, bladder, and other organs. If a pregnant woman smokes, she runs the risk of hurting her unborn child. Children born to mothers who smoke weigh less and get sick more often than other children.

Breathing in other people's smoke (called second-hand smoking) is also unhealthy. Many studies show that this kind of passive smoking causes lung and heart diseases as well as cancer. People who live with smokers tend to be sick more often than people who live in smoke-free homes.

More than 1,000 people die every day from illnesses due to tobacco products. Millions more get sick from smoking or using tobacco in other ways. That's the bad news.

The good news is that smokers can quit. In many cases, the damage done by smoking can be reversed. But years of smoking can do permanent damage to the body. When that happens, nothing can be done about it. And it happens too often. The average smoker lives six to eight years less than a non-smoker. Six to eight years is a lot of time to lose just for a cigarette.

44

Caffeine, Caffeine, Caffeine

It's early in the morning: time for you to get to school, time for Mom and Dad to get to work. You let out a groan: "Oh, I can't wake up. Do I have to go to school today?" You drag yourself out of bed, throw on some clothes, and walk into the kitchen.

"Morning," you manage to mumble to your family. Your father is reading the newspaper and sipping a cup of coffee. Your mother is looking over some papers from the office. She's on her second cup of coffee. And your little sister has settled down to a breakfast of chocolate-flavored cereal.

"Breakfast?" your mother asks.

"No," you answer. "Just a doughnut," you grumble as you reach for the chocolate ones on the kitchen table.

"Is that any way to start the day?" your father asks.

That's a good question. What kind of way *is* this to start the day?

The answer is that it's a drug-assisted way. The drug your family is depending on to get the day started is caffeine. The coffee, the chocolate-flavored cereal, and the chocolate doughnut: these are all products with caffeine in them. So is the chocolate milk you have with lunch, the candy bar and soda you have after school, and the iced tea you drink with dinner. All of these have caffeine in them.

Like other drugs, caffeine changes the way we think and feel and behave. Like other drugs, it can be habit forming. But unlike many other drugs, caffeine is an everyday drug.

Caffeine is not as harmful to the body as other drugs. It is not as addictive. But it is a strong drug, and it can be a real problem for both adults and young people.

The problem is that it is easy to get too much caffeine.

- It's easy because we usually don't even think of caffeine as a drug. "What's the harm of another cup of coffee?" you might ask. Or, "Why not have another soda?"

- It's easy because products with caffeine are just about everywhere. They are not illegal. They are not only for adults. Caffeine products are as nearby as the closest grocery store or soda machine.

- It's easy because caffeine is in so many different products. Caffeine is in certain aspirin products, cold medicines, and diet pills. People who want to cut back on caffeine often find themselves using caffeine products without even knowing it.

It is especially easy for young people to get too much caffeine. Their bodies are smaller, so even a small amount of caffeine has a big effect on them. And caffeine products are part of daily life for most kids. They are allowed to eat and drink many foods with caffeine. They can get as much caffeine from sodas and candy bars as adults get from coffee and tea.

How to Quit the Caffeine Habit

Do you need caffeine to start the day? Do you need a caffeine lift in the afternoon? Do you feel run-down if you don't get your daily dose of caffeine?

If your answer is "Yes" to questions like these, you probably have a caffeine habit. There's never any better time to stop it than now. Here are some helpful tips on how to get caffeine out of your life:

- Cut back on sodas and candy bars.

- Switch to caffeine-free sodas.

- Try fruit juices instead of soft drinks.

- Try hard candy instead of chocolate.

- Ask your parents to use medicines without caffeine.

- Use carob products instead of chocolate.

- Try chewing sugar-free gum instead of chocolate candy.

- Switch to herbal teas.

What Is Caffeine?

The best way not to get too much caffeine is to know what it is and what it does to us. Only then will you be able to say "No" to the caffeine habit.

Caffeine is a bitter-tasting, odorless drug found in many different kinds of plants. It has been used for thousands of years in countries throughout the world.

There are four well known sources of caffeine:

-- Coffee beans
   -- Tea leaves
      -- Cocoa beans
         -- Cola nuts

From these sources, we get such everyday products as coffee, tea, chocolate, and cola drinks. These products have different amounts of caffeine in them. We measure caffeine in units of weight called milligrams.

• Coffee beans

Coffee and products made with coffee are one of the most popular ways to use caffeine. Most people drink coffee as a hot beverage. A steaming coffee pot can be found in many homes, most offices, and almost all restaurants. In the United States and Canada, over 100 million people drink coffee. The average American drinks over three cups of coffee a day.

Coffee is made from the beans of the coffee tree. The beans are dried and roasted; then, the roasted beans are ground into coffee particles. Depending on how the coffee particles are brewed, one 6-ounce cup of coffee contains between 80 and 150 milligrams of caffeine.

Besides being used to make this popular beverage, coffee beans are also used to flavor ice cream, baked goods, candy, yogurt, and other products.

Coffee comes from the Middle East. It has been a popular drink there for over 500 years. In the 1500s and 1600s, the use of coffee as a beverage spread throughout the world. Then, in the 1720s, the coffee tree was introduced to the South American country of Brazil. Today, Brazil is the largest coffee producer in the world. But there are many other countries that produce coffee in Central and South America, Asia, and Africa.

• Tea leaves

Tea is another popular caffeine beverage. It is made from the leaves of the tea plant. The tea plant grows well in warm and rainy climates. Many of the major tea-producing countries are in Asia: China, Japan, India, Pakistan, Sri Lanka, Bangladesh, and Indonesia. But countries in Africa, the Middle East, and South America produce tea, too.

No one knows who made the first cup of tea, but the use of tea as a beverage is thousands of years old. Drinking tea probably started in China and spread from there to Japan, India, and other countries in Asia. It was not until the mid 1600s that Dutch and British traders brought tea leaves back with them from their journeys to Asia. Soon after that, tea became a very popular drink throughout the world. Today, tea is the most widely used hot beverage in the world.

Like coffee beans, tea leaves are brewed with hot water to make a caffeine beverage. There are different kinds of tea drinks, depending on where the tea plants are grown, what kinds of tea leaves are used, and how the leaves are prepared. One 6-ounce cup of tea (brewed for about three minutes) contains between 20 and 40 milligrams of caffeine.

• Cocoa beans

Chocolate! Just the sound of it makes your mouth water. Chocolate cake, chocolate ice cream, chocolate candy: there are so many different ways to enjoy it. But chocolate is a caffeine product, too. It is one of the most popular ways young people use caffeine.

Chocolate is made from the beans of the cocoa tree. When the beans are ground, they produce a dark brown liquid called chocolate liquor. Chocolate factories make many different products by adding milk, sugar, and other ingredients to the chocolate liquor. A chocolate candy bar contains about 50 to 75 milligrams of caffeine.

The first people to make chocolate from the beans of the cocoa plant were probably the Maya and Aztec Indians of Central America. They used chocolate to make a cold drink called cachuatl. In the 1500s, Spanish explorers tried the drink for themselves. They added sugar to the Indian brew and served it hot. The new drink was called chocolatl. Chocolatl soon became a popular beverage in Spain, and its use spread to other countries as well. Today, the United States makes more chocolate than any country in the world. It also uses the most chocolate—over 300,000 tons of chocolate are consumed each year in the United States.

• Cola nuts

The nuts of the cola tree are used to make cola sodas. The cola tree comes from western Africa, but it is now grown in Asia and South America, too.

Cola nuts were first used to flavor soft drinks in 1888. In that year, John Styth Pemberton, a pharmacist from Atlanta, Georgia, developed a drink with a syrup made from the nuts of the cola tree. He advertised his new beverage as "The New and Popular Soda Fountain Drink, containing the famous cola nuts." He called it Coca-Cola. Before long, this new drink was a big hit. By 1902, Coca-Cola was the most well known product in America.

One 12-ounce serving of Coca-Cola contains about 48 milligrams (48 mg) of caffeine. Many other soft drinks contain caffeine, too: Mountain Dew (54 mg), RC Cola (48 mg), TAB (47 mg), Diet Coke (46 mg), Dr. Pepper (41 mg), and Pepsi-Cola (36 mg) are just a few of them. (Today, there are also many caffeine-free soft drinks for people who like their sodas without drugs.)

No wonder caffeine is an everyday drug. It's in so many different things. The problem is what happens when caffeine gets inside us. Now that we know what caffeine is, let's see what it does to us.

What Does Caffeine Do?

From an early morning cup of coffee to a bedtime drink of hot chocolate or cocoa: we use caffeine products all day long. Caffeine is so much a part of our lives that we don't even think of it as a drug.

But it is. Like many other drugs, it changes the way we think, feel, and behave. And like all drugs, it can be harmful.

Caffeine speeds up the way the brain and body work. It speeds up the heart rate and breathing. It makes people feel more alert and gives them a boost of energy. People say it gives them a "kick" that gets them going. They say that, with caffeine, they work more quickly and think more clearly.

Caffeine is a habit-forming drug. The brain gets used to the caffeine kick and depends on a steady dose of it. Many caffeine users can't get the day started without a cup of coffee or some other caffeine product. Others need an afternoon caffeine "lift" to get them through the day.

The caffeine kick may get people going, but it won't keep them going for long. Caffeine stays in the body only for a short while. Once the caffeine kick is over, users often feel tired and sluggish. They feel upset and irritable. And they feel that they need more caffeine.

The regular use of caffeine, like the regular use of many other drugs, can lead to tolerance. Users then need more and more caffeine to get the same effect they used to get from a smaller amount. So what do they do? They may have an extra cup of coffee or tea. They may drink one cola after another. But what they are really doing is beginning to develop a harmful caffeine habit.

Too much caffeine can make it hard for people to think clearly and concentrate. It causes headaches, muscle tremors, and stomach problems. It makes people nervous and jittery. This is sometimes called "coffee nerves" or "coffee jitters." It may have more serious effects. Studies have linked caffeine to heart disease, certain kinds of cancer, and birth defects.

How much caffeine is too much?

The effect of caffeine is not the same on everybody. So it is hard to say how much caffeine is too much. But doctors say that adults should not drink more than two cups of coffee a day. A cup of brewed coffee has about 80 to 150 milligrams of caffeine. (A cup of instant coffee has less caffeine.) That means that an adult should have no more than 300 milligrams of caffeine a day. And young people should have much less than that.

How Much Is Too Much?

How much caffeine do you use each day? To help you measure how much caffeine you use, here's a chart of some everyday products and the amount of caffeine they contain:

Food or Product:	Caffeine (in milligrams):
Coffee (6 ounces)	
brewed	80-150
instant	40-65
Hot tea (6 ounces)	20-40
Iced tea (12 ounces)	67-76
Soda (12 ounces)	36-54
Chocolate candy (1 ounce)	10-30
Chocolate cake (small slice)	20-30
Chocolate milk (5 ounces)	2-15
Pain relievers (1 tablet)	32-65

Add up how much caffeine you use in a single day. You may be in for a big surprise. Those sodas, candy bars, and other caffeine products can add up very quickly to too much caffeine. Some young people, in fact, are using more caffeine than is safe even for adults.

People who use caffeine to get energy are also hurting themselves in another way. Often, they do not get other, more healthy sources of energy. A good breakfast is a better way to start the day than a chocolate doughnut. The right foods give you energy that lasts, and without harmful effects. But many people choose the quick kick of caffeine instead.

Also, many caffeine products, like soda and chocolate, contain large amounts of sugar. Like caffeine, sugar gives people a short burst of energy. This adds to the kick of caffeine products. But, also like caffeine, the effect of sugar wears off quickly. This adds to the feeling of tiredness that caffeine users get. Caffeine and sugar are a doubly bad combination.

People say you are what you eat. They mean that what you eat and drink affects everything about you: how you look and how you feel. If you want to be and do your best, the best thing is to use as little caffeine as possible.

Everyday Drugs
and You

Now you know the facts about nicotine and caffeine.

You know how these drugs change the way we think, feel, and behave. You know what they do to the body and what they do to the brain.

You also know that nicotine and caffeine are everyday drugs. You know that you will grow up in a world where these drugs are used by many people.

And you know that you will have to make a decision about these drugs. You will have to decide whether or not to use nicotine and caffeine.

What should you do?

What should you decide to do about these everyday drugs?

Say "No" to Nicotine

If you think about the facts, you will say "No" to nicotine. It makes the people who use it sick. It even hurts those who do not use it. It is very addictive. You may not be able to stop using it when you want to. And, for young people, it is against the law to buy tobacco products.

But knowing the facts doesn't always make it easy to say "No" to drugs. It isn't easy to say "No" to nicotine when your friends are smoking and when they want you to smoke, too.

You *can* say "No." It takes a little courage. It takes a little practice. But you can do it. Here are some ways to say "No" that may work for you:

"No. Smoking makes people sick."

"No. I'm too busy."

"No. I hate the way it smells."

"No. It's against the law."

"No. I like to be able to breathe."

"No. Let's do something else instead."

"No. I thought you had more sense than that."

You can think of other ways to say "No." You can practice saying "No" before you really need to. You can make friends with people who don't smoke.

You can do what's right for you.

Cut Down on Caffeine

Caffeine is not as strong a drug as nicotine, and it is not as dangerous. But now that you know the facts about caffeine, you know that getting too much caffeine can be harmful.

And you know how easy it is to get too much caffeine. It's easy because caffeine is in so many different products.

But you can control the amount of caffeine you use. You can be smart about what you buy. You can watch what you eat. You can cut back on sodas and candy bars.

Look for the words "caffeine-free" on the products you eat and drink. These words will lead you to products that keep the good taste you want and leave out the caffeine you don't need. They will help you say "No" to too much caffeine.

Knowing about drugs is one way you can take control of your health and your happiness. Although you probably hear more about drugs like cocaine and marijuana, it is important to remember that nicotine and caffeine are drugs, too. It is also important to remember that everything you eat and drink affects your health. So be smart. Say "No" to tobacco products. Cut down on caffeine. Take control of your life and make it a drug-free one!

Glossary

addiction the constant need or craving that makes people use drugs they know are harmful

alveoli tiny airsacs in the lungs through which oxygen and carbon dioxide travel

bronchial tubes the two large airways that lead from the trachea to the lungs

bronchioles the small airways in the lungs

caffeine a drug found in such products as coffee, tea, cola drinks, and chocolate

cancer a disease that attacks and destroys healthy body tissues

carbon monoxide one of the poisonous gases found in tobacco smoke

cilia tiny, hairlike cells that help move mucus out of the lungs

dependence the way the body and brain need a drug to avoid feeling sick

drug a substance that changes the way the brain works

gateway drug	a drug that can lead to other drug problems
hydrogen cyanide	one of the poisonous gases found in tobacco smoke
mucus	a thick, sticky fluid that traps dirt and other particles in the lungs
nicotine	a drug found in the leaves of the tobacco plant
peer pressure	the feeling that you have to do something because other people your age are doing it
second-hand smoking	breathing in other people's smoke; also called passive smoking
stimulant	a kind of drug that speeds up the way the brain works
tar	a gummy paste made up of chemicals produced by tobacco smoke
tobacco	the plant from which nicotine comes
tolerance	the way the body and brain need more and more of a drug to get the same effect
trachea	the tube that leads from the throat to the lungs; also called the windpipe
withdrawal	the sick feeling drug users get when they can't get the drugs they are dependent on

Index